TATTING
ARTISTRY IN THREAD
HELMA SIEPMANN
TRANSLATED FROM GERMAN BY ETHA SCHUETTE

LACIS
PUBLICATIONS
BERKELEY, CALIFORNIA USA

ARTISTRY IN TATTING
is
the new craft
for young and old
for those who love nature.

She transforms everybody, who admits to her, into an artist
Free after Goethe:

"Wem sich die Natur erschließt,
der greift zu ihrer würdigsten Auslegerin

- der Kunst -"

This book is a translation of the
Original German language manuscript by Helma Siepmann
English translation by Etha Schuette
Rights on all samples by Helma Siepmann
© 2004, Helma Siepmann

© 2004 English text. Lacis Publications

LACIS
PUBLICATIONS
3163 ADELINE STREET
BERKELEY, CA 94703

ISBN 1-891656-53-8

CONTENTS

PREFACE

THE NATURE OF ARTISTRY IN TATTING

The art of tatting, as a form of lace, has been practiced for generations in all parts of the world. For a long time it was the needlework of choice for noble societies. It has now again become common to work filigree laces and a multitude of decorations with shuttle and thread.

In general, the fabrication of this lace demands a constant duplication of pattern repeats. To work from a pattern one has to work with exact instructions and count the numbers of stitches for the *Rings* and *Picots* and their connections to each other.

ARTISTRY IN TATTING INVOLVES A COMPLETELY DIFFERENT APPROACH

Never are there any original repetitions or copies, only similarities.

With the basic techniques – developed from the classical form of tatting – and the play with new forms of knots, viz. *the Creative Stitch,* and 5 new knotted elements, everybody can form their own tatted artistry in thread. Here, one does not follow geometric patterns as in lace making but rather forms the tatting according to the shapes of nature, with her incredible multitude of flower and leaf shapes, trees, shrubs and landscapes.

It is not important to copy all elements true to nature. It rather happens by itself that one captures the essence of a plant or a tree. And, whoever believes that they do not have enough talent for this kind of work, rest assured that most things considered to be a mistake can be turned around and seen as a creative innovation that fits into the scheme. This is how your imagination gets animated and you practice creativity.

In this second book I give you the basic technique for using 2 shuttles, 5 new knotting elements and instructions on how to work with three shuttles. I suggest that the reader practice the lessons in order, step by step. In the end you will have your own design. Each of the 5 chapter lessons begins with a playful introduction to the respective knotting element, usually in the form of working flowering plants which can be used for greeting or table cards or small pictures and appliques for clothing and table centers. Further examples include ideas for pictorial representations, some in connection with silk painting.

This way every tatter can chose their own preferences and way of working an artistic approach to tatting.

I wish you, the reader, a lot of fun with this new thread technique and many beautiful ideas for your continuing work.

Hattingen, summer 2003
Helma Siepmann

SUPPLIES

You will need a shuttle for tatting, the tool to hold and facilitate manipulation of your thread. Shuttles are available in many variations and materials.

This is a small collection of wood, plastic and metal shuttles, with or without a hook, and two tatting hooks, one of which has a finger ring and chain. The hooks are used in traditional tatting to connect adjacent *Rings* or *Chains*.

For tatted artistry an ordinary crochet hook will be useful in addition to the mini tatting hooks because for some designs it is necessary to over-crochet or gather several picots at the same time.

Any type of thread can be used: cotton crochet thread and perle cotton of all sizes, and fine lace threads, such as 35/2 or 60/2 linen which is available in many colors. Several plies wound together of very thin sewing thread or fine metallic threads can also be suitable materials. Wool can be used with caution. You should avoid blends as a mixture with synthetic yarns will reduce the yarn's elasticity. The latter is important for closing *rings* completely and tightly. A suggested beginner's thread is #5 or #8 perle cotton.

Forceps are practical to use when elements are to be glued onto paper. Use a glue that doesn't pull threads such as a millinery glue. To attach appliques to fabric use an iron-on fusible web such as *"HeatnBond ®"* or *"Trans-Web®."*

Instruction for working with iron-on fusible web:
   1. protect ironing board with paper and lay tatted piece face down
   2. Iron on the web following manufacturer's directions.
   3. Roughly cut out all pieces and peel off protective paper.
   4. Iron on the coated tatting, working the tip of the iron into all corners and spaces
   5. If need be repeat step 4.
   The application should be machine washable.

To make a picture with a silk background, without adhesive, pad the silk with foam. Then lay your tatted elements loosely onto the silk and fix them with glass and frame, compressing the padding. On a non-silk fabric background, the tatted elements will stick sufficiently so that there is no need for foam padding.

THE BASIC TECHNIQUES

To wind thread onto the shuttle, lead the thread end through the small hole in the center and make a knot. Now hold the shuttle sideways and wind the thread around the core until the shuttle is full, without causing the points to separate.

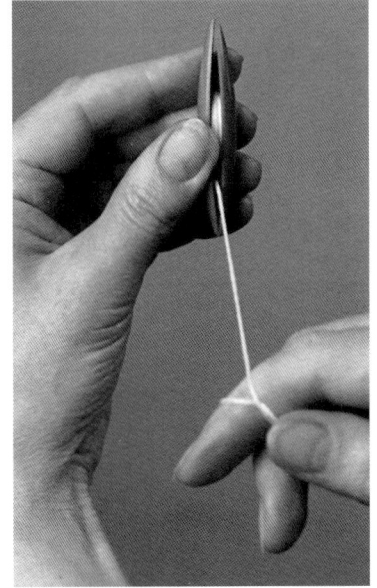

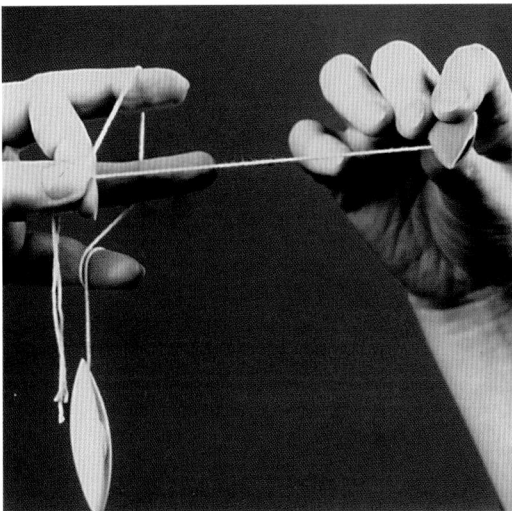

To practice, it is best to use two shuttles with the two threads knotted together. Hold the knot with thumb and index finger of your left hand and throw one of the threads over the other fingers of the left hand. Hold the second shuttle in your right hand in a way that the thread leaves the shuttle from the front half, away from your body.

The ring finger of your right hand now pulls the shuttle thread back and the middle finger lifts the shuttle thread up, working as in the following illustrations.

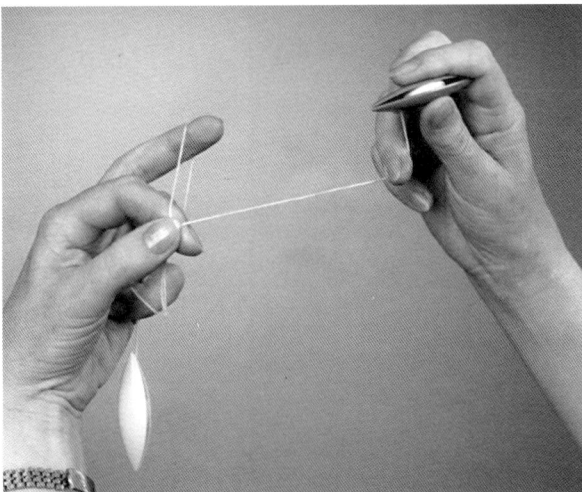

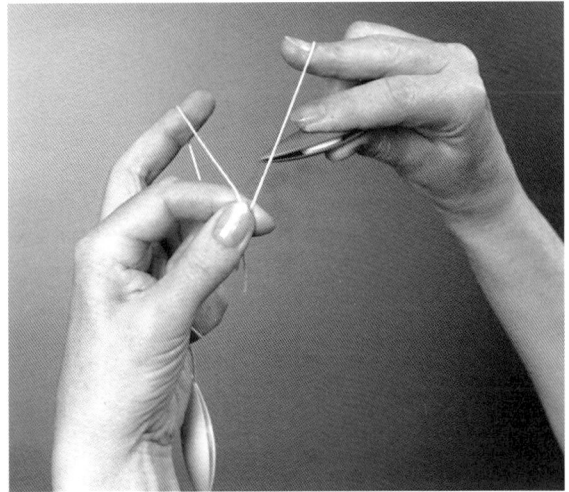

THE *REVERSE KNOT*

Lead the shuttle under both threads, and back between both threads.

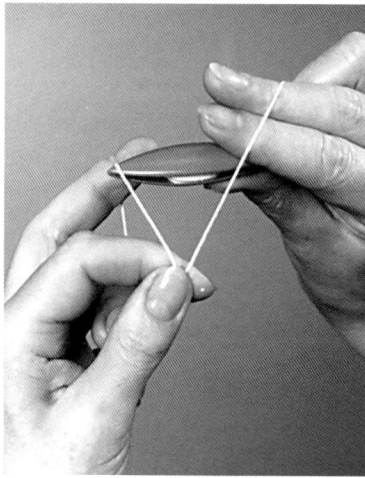

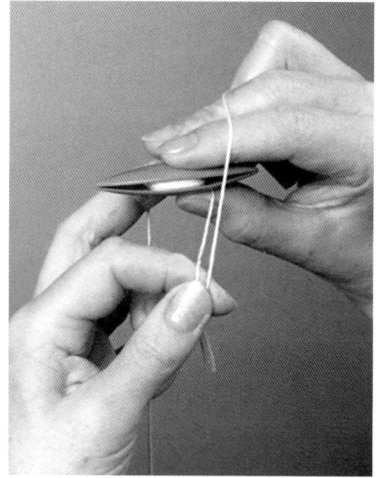

Here you have to keep the left thread taut so that the knot doesn't flip over.

This is how you work the first half of the *Reverse Knot*.

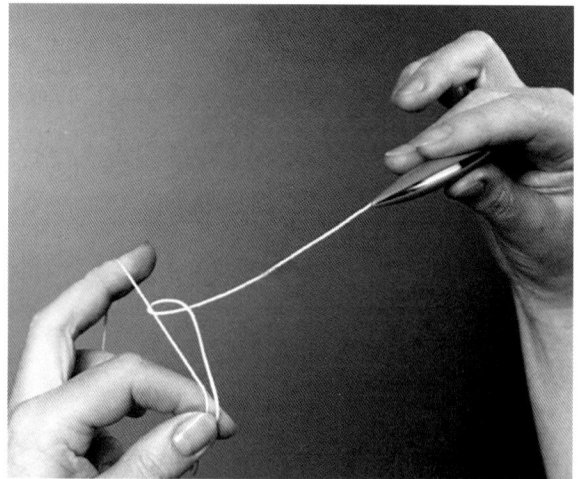

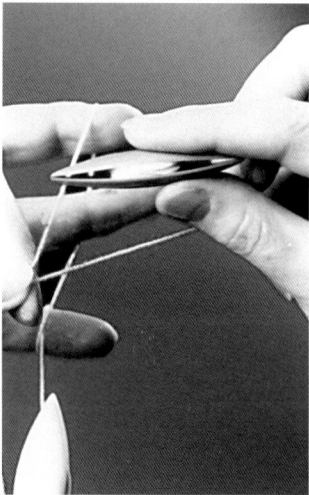

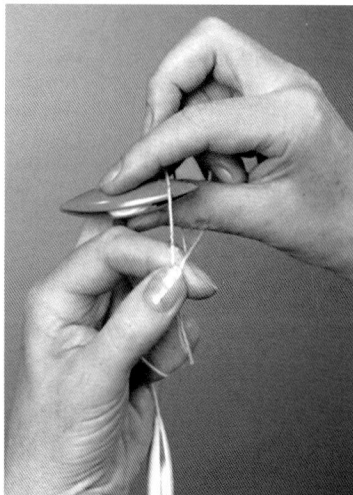

Proceed in opposite manner for the second half: Lead the shuttle first over the left thread, then back and under it.

The *Reverse Knot* is completed!

Note: With this knot keep the left thread taut at all times! The thread in the shuttle will be the visible thread.

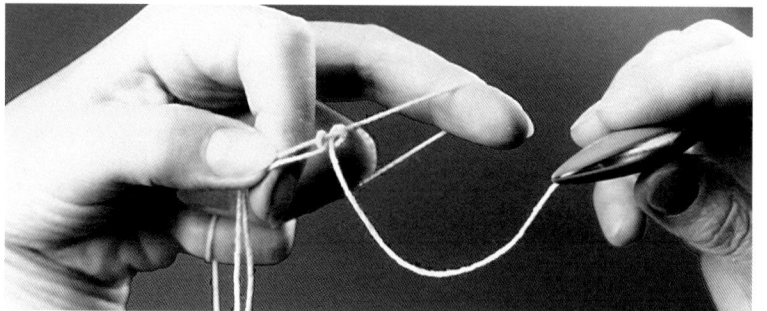

THE *DOUBLE KNOT*

This knot also consists of a left and a right half. This knot will be formed by the left thread, in contrast to the *Reverse Knot*. For this, keep the left thread relaxed after pulling the shuttle back until the right thread is tightened again. Lifting the middle finger now, while keeping the right thread taut, will cause the knot to slip under the thumb and has to be held there until the second half of the knot is done.

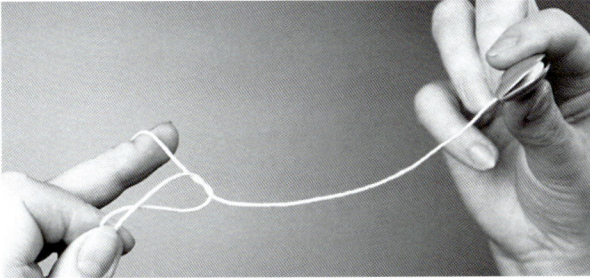

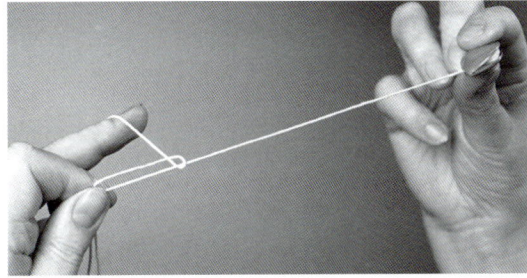

THE TRADITIONAL
DOUBLE KNOT

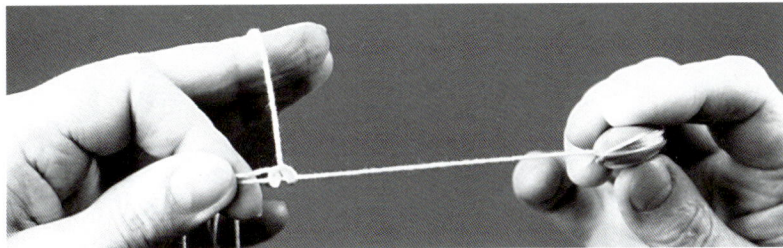

FIRST EXERCISES

Knot together threads of two colors and work alternating:

3 Double Knots / 3 Reverse Knots

2 Double Knots / 2 Reverse Knots

1 Double Knot / 1 Reverse Knot

½ *Double Knot* / ½ *Reverse Knot*. This knot is typically used at the beginning and end of all creative work to secure the other stitches and is thus called the *Creative Knot*.

Both *green* and *yellow* threads are the core and come from the left hand. You knot with *red* in the right hand: 3 *Double Knots* / 3 *Reverse Knots*

Working with the same colors but *red* and *green* are now the core in the left hand and the knotting is done with *yellow*. 3 *Double Knots* / 3 *Reverse Knots*

A variation with 2 *Double Knots* and 2 *Reverse Knots*.

In the top row knotting was done in *red* over the *green* and *yellow* core threads in the left hand. The bottom shows knotting with *green* over the *red* and *yellow* core threads from the left hand.

A variation of (1) *Double Knot* of *red* and *green* combined and (1) *green Reverse Knot*.

A variation with the *Creative Knot*: left *Double Knot* with *red* and *yellow*; right *Reverse Knot* with *green*.

THREAD COMPARISONS

Perle Cotton

Wool

Silk Ribbon

Novelty Thread

THE *KNOTS* AND THEIR USES

The *Double Knot*:

Worked with one shuttle only and is used in connection with *Picots* in all round elements (left and right conventional knot (*See pg. 5).

The *Reverse Knot*:

Worked with at least 2 shuttles for making linear elements (left and right *Reverse Knot*. *See pg. 4).

The *Creative Knot* (sometimes referred to as a *Lock Stitch*) with 2 threads:

This is used to join a new thread and at the beginning and ending of all work (left *Conventional Knot* and right *Reverse Knot*).

The *Creative Knot* with 3 threads:

Begin work with this knot. It is relatively thick (it should be hidden while pasting on or ironing on).

The *Split Creative Knot*:

Used to secure 3-thread work, because it is less bulky: For the first half use only one thread of the left hand as the core, for the second half work the knot over both threads of the left hand.

The *Thread Scissors*:

Used primarily to tie up chains in order to close a round. Insert and clamp preworked flower chains or leaves between the two core threads and then close these threads with a *Reverse Knot*. (*See pg 10)

THE *PICOT*

Leaving a space between two *Double Knots* and then sliding them together forms the *Picot*. The same occurs between two *Reverse Knots*. Here it will point downwards and is called *Reverse Picot*.

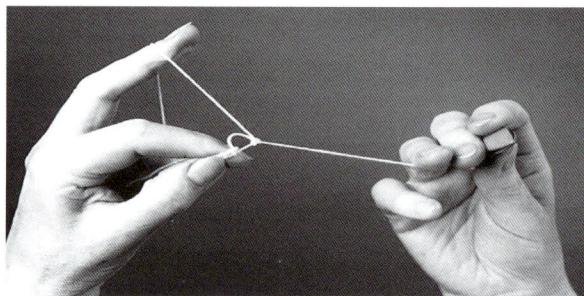

A 2-shuttle exercise with *Picots* and *Reverse Picots*. The yellow *Picots* point upwards, the green *Reverse Picots* point downwards.

THE *RING*
1-shuttle work

All round knotted elements (rings) are worked with one shuttle only. For this, lead the shuttle thread around the fingers of the left hand and ...

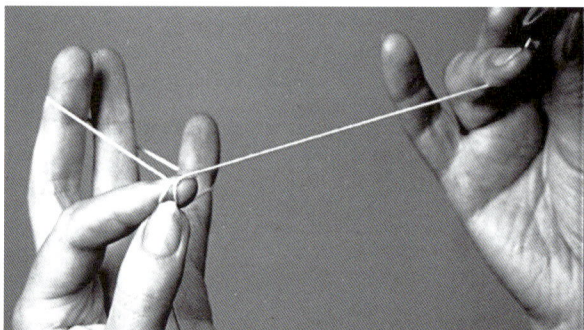

...pull the ring closed after making the knots.

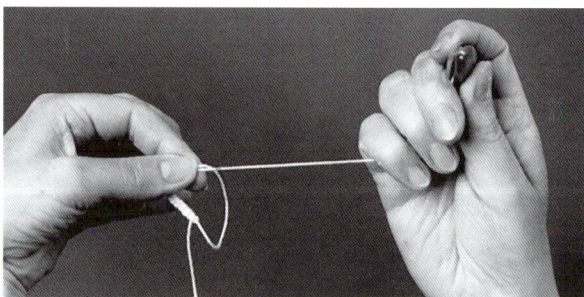

Note: Round knotted elements are: the Josephine Ring, *the* Shells, *the* Picot Ring, *the* Over-Crocheted Picot Ring *and the* Gathered Picot Ring.

All of these can be used for blossoms, leaves, berries, buds, etc.

Start with a *Creative Knot,* in which two threads, red and
brown, are held by the left hand and the third, green thread, is used for knotting.

Now start with the blossom, in this case a *Picot Ring.* Knot the
stem and then follow with closely worked ground leaves, in this example two
large *Picot Rings* with varying sizes of *Picots.*

Lay the two *Picot Rings* on top of each other flipping
one upwards and work the second stem and the second
blossom. Finish with a *Split Creative Knot.*

Beginning and ending threads can now be cut off short.

Bring the plant into the desired shape when gluing or ironing it
onto the ground material. Hide the *Creative Knots* at the back of
the work.

FLOWER BASICS
3-shuttle work

Example of a flower from *Josephine Rings (See pg. 13):*

Start with a *Creative Knot,* in which two threads are held by the left hand and the third shuttle (green thread) is used for knotting.

Use the flower color to knot a round element (here it is a *Josephine Ring*).

Use the second shuttle to knot (brown thread) over the two other threads (on the left hand) one *Reverse Knot* (for larger blossoms use a *Reverse*) for the pistil.

Repeat *Josephine Ring / Reverse Knot* at least 4 - 6 times.

Now put the *Reverse Knot* thread (brown) in front of the first flower petal and work a second *Reverse Knot* behind it over both other threads. This closes the round of flower petals. In other words: You clamp the first petal into the so called *Thread Scissors. (See pg. 7).*

Now pull on the unused third thread, green, to neatly close the round and pistil, this thread referred to as the *Pull Thread.*

10

Working with a Picot Gauge

For very accurate work, which is not really necessary as nature is not too measured, and to work the *Gathered Picot Ring (See Part IV)* a picot gauge is a useful tool. The gauge can be a length of stiff cardboard, plastic or wood cut to an appropriate width. To use:

Start with a double knot, put the picot gauge into the crossing threads of left and right side, that is, behind the working thread.

Work the next knot at the lower edge of the gauge.

Fetch and put the working thread again in front of the gauge and continue on in this manner...

...until you complete the required number of *Picots*.

Remove the picot gauge and close the ring.

Note: for the Gathered Picot Ring *you must secure it first with a* Right Knot *(See pg. 86).*

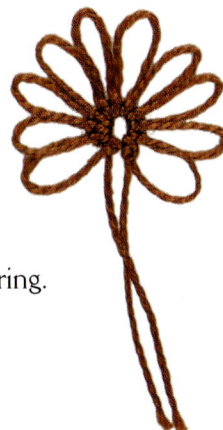

NEW IDEAS IN TATTING
PART I

WORKING WITH *JOSEPHINE RINGS, SHELLS* AND *PICOT RINGS*

SIMPLE ROUND KNOTTED ELEMENTS
1-shuttle work

THE *JOSEPHINE RING*

A series of right knots pulled together into a ring
Application: for all sorts of leaves and petals

15 Knots   *20 Knots*

FLOWER

Blossom and stem leaves of *Josephine Rings*
(*See pg. 10 for instructions for flower*)

THE *CHAIN OF JOSEPHINE RINGS*

A series of *Josephine Rings* worked in continuous fashion.
Application: for all sorts of foliage

FLORAL EXAMPLES

1. Blossom as shown above, stem of *Reverse Knots* over red and yellow
Ground foliage: a *Chain of Josephine Rings*, starting with large ones, then
gradually smaller ones.

2. Ground foliage worked in two parts: first a *Chain of Josephine Rings* with *Reverse Knots* over red and yellow threads (of the left hand) tied together, then a second *Josephine Ring Chain* worked as before and tied to the stem, then the 2nd stem of *Reverse Knots* over red and yellow and finally a blossom as before.

TENDRILS

1. Blossoms as before, leaves left and right: two *Josephine Rings* worked closely after each other and tied together with *Reverse Knots* over the red and yellow threads. Center leaf: *Chain of Josephine Rings.*

2. A round leaf is formed by a *Gathered Chain of Josephine Rings* made by tying the *Chain of Josephine Rings* back to the stem with a *Thread Scissor* and *Reverse Knot, here* over the red and yellow threads.

BLOSSOM VARIATIONS

1. Star blossom: five *Josephine Rings* with *Picot*

2. Star blossom tendril: work the flowers from six *Josephine Rings* with *Picot;* the leaves of three *Josephine Rings* of 20 right knots (thus, larger than before) tied together with *Reverse Knots* over the red and yellow threads, in continuous fashion.

3. Five flower petals of triple *Josephine Rings*:
   a. Work three *Josephine Rings* (bottom left),
   b. fold the last *Josephine Ring* back onto the other two (center left) and work ½ yellow *Reverse Knot* over red and green,
   c. repeat both four times (center right) and
   d. close the flower ring as usual (right) with the *Thread Scissors*.

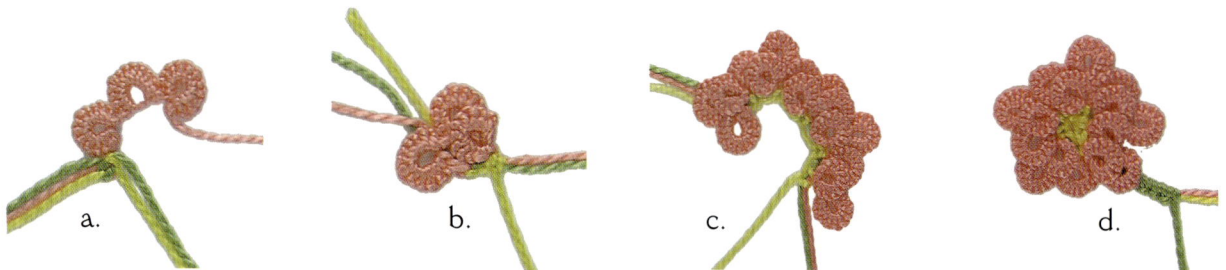

a.

b.

c.

d.

Hint: All these patterns can similarly be worked from Shells. *They will appear a bit softer (see next page). It is easier to work with* Josephine Rings, *because* Shells *have to be knotted rather loosely.*

14

THE *SHELLS* (*MUSSEL RINGS*)

All left knots pulled into a ring, otherwise
same as *Josephine Ring*
Application: for all sorts of leaves and petals

THE CHAIN OF SHELLS

Many *Shells* worked consecutively
Application: for all sorts of foliage.

Examples (as previously shown in
Josephine Rings).

TENDRIL OF ASSORTED ELEMENTS

Outer blossoms and inner leaf made from *Shells* and
inner blossoms and outer leaves from *Josephine Rings*

VARIATIONS

1. Work the blossom with six or seven petals instead of five.
2. Work the pistil with *Reverse Picots* instead of *Reverse Knots*.
3. Mix *Josephine Rings* and *Shells* in one flower to change their relation within each blossom
   as well as their relation to each other from one blossom to the next.
4. Work with variegated or overdyed thread creating light and shadow effects.

15

EXAMPLES FOR FLORAL VARIATIONS WITH JOSEPHINE RINGS

Floral fundamentals: 3 shuttles required, as shown below in the basic example: one for the flower buds (or berries), one for the stem and one for the ground leaves.

Always start at the tip with a *Creative Knot*, work the stem, then the ground leaves and then the second stem. Finish with a *Split Creative Knot. The 3 shuttles can also be used differently as shown in the following examples.*

BASIC EXAMPLE:

Creative Knot (two threads on left hand)

> BERRY: * red *Josephine Ring.*
>
> STEM: Six *Reverse Knots* over red and green
> Repeat: from * four times.
>
> GROUND LEAVES:
>
> 1. *Chain of Josephine Rings.* Tie with *Reverse Knots* to the other two threads.
> 2. *Chain of Josephine Rings* worked like the first one.
>
> STEM: Seven *Reverse Knots.*
>
> BERRY: ** *Josephine Ring.*
>
> STEM: Two *Reverse Knots.*
>
> Repeat: from ** five times.
>
> FINISH: *Split Creative Knot.*
> Cut thread ends short.

VARIATION 1

In this example the pull-thread inside the stem is beige, hence it is not visible, but it gives you the opportunity to straighten out the stem while working on it.

There are always two *Josephine Rings* worked right after one another, then tied together with a *Reverse Knot* for the stems.

Position the rings on left and right sides of the stem.

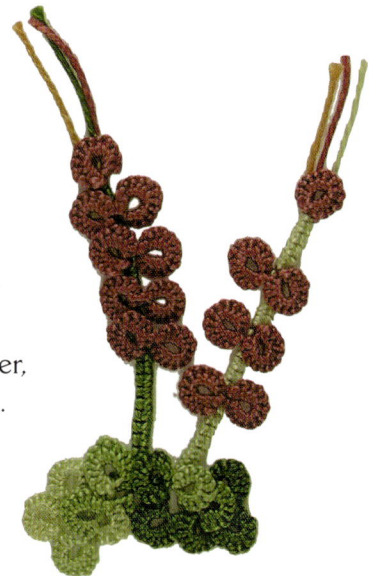

16

Variation 2

In contrast to the previous example, three *Josephine Rings* were knotted closely together and the third one folded backwards.

Variation 3

Same as Variation 2, but here the number of the green *Reverse Knots* making up the stem was reduced step by step to generate more density at the bottom.

Variation 4

Similar to *Variation 3*, but here the triple *Josephine Rings* were worked with increasing number of knots and always arranged opposite each other. At the tip there are three *Josephine Rings* with 10 *Half Knots*, then three with 12, then 14, 16, 18 and at the end 20 *Half Knots*. At the same time the number of the green *Reverse Knots* increases in steps from an initial 3 to finally 6 *Half Knots*.

  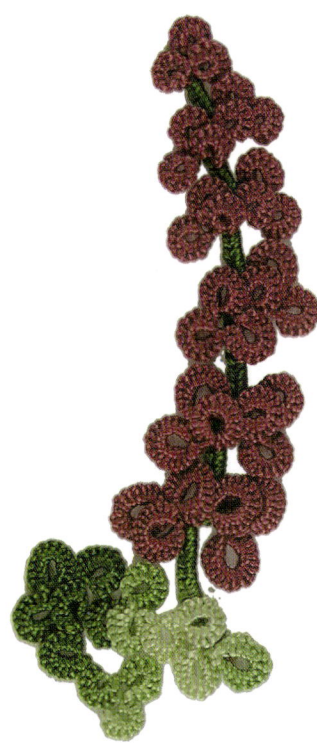

| VARIATION 2 | VARIATION 3 | VARIATION 4 |

Other Variations

1. Change the stem intervals by varying the number of *Reverse Knots*.
2. Place the *Josephine Rings* on one side of the stem only.
3. Put a *Picot* inside each *Josephine Ring*.
4. Work *Shells* instead of *Josephine Rings*.
5. Place single green *Josephine Rings* between the red ones for stem leaves.

DESIGN SUGGESTIONS (*For applique with iron-on web*)

1. Single blossom/leaf elements in light green, variegated red and dark brown threads.

Start with a green *Chain of Josephine Rings*, then add red with a *Creative Knot* and work the first red *Josephine Ring*. Now add the brown thread with a *Reverse Knot* over green and red, which forms the first knot for the pistil. Repeat the *Josephine Ring* and *Reverse Knot* another four times. Cut off the brown and red threads close to the work and knot another *Chain of Josephine Rings*. Pull the last ring tight and cut off remaining thread. Iron on with adhesive. *(See pg. 2)*.

2. A tendril of blooms in variegated red, light green and dark brown thread.

Worked in similar fashion as previous example, but here work is done continuously, i.e. *Reverse Knots* cover the red and green threads after each blossom or leaf to make the stem. The green *Chains of Josephine Rings* are always tied back to the stem *(See pg. 14)*. Note: *The leaves will arrange themselves in a pleasing manner without much effort to create a natural appearance. In addition, the blossoms are worked singly or in double and triple groups. These variations further add to the natural appearance of the tendril.*

3. DECORATIVE TABLE BAND

Here two tendrils with three blossoms and three leaves come from left and right to meet in the center with a fourth blossom. Two additional blossoms, arranged above and below the tendril ends, make up a new motif in the center. For the stems, red and brown threads are covered with green *Reverse Knots*.

18

4. DECORATIVE TABLE BAND

Variegated thread was used for the yellow and green elements. Brown thread was used for the pistils and the stems. The *Chains of Josephine Rings* are longer than in the previous example and tied back onto the stem. When worked in this way, the tendril attains an especially natural appearance.

5. DECORATIVE TABLE BAND

Some blossoms are made from light purple thread and some from dark purple thread. In several blossoms both colors were mixed. The pistils were worked in *Reverse Picots* with doubled metallic gold thread. To the left and right of the round of blossoms there is a tendril made up of blossoms and a stem, which bears leaves at a distance of two triple *Josephine Rings* (first work 3 consecutive *Josephine Rings*, tie them together with a green half *Reverse Knot* over the pink and gold threads and then work the next three in mirror fashion). Single blossoms, partly with or without stems, were added during the ironing onto the band.

19

More design suggestions with *Josephine Ring* flowers that were knotted with and without *Picots* and arranged during the ironing with adhesive.

A picture made exclusively from *Chains of Josephine Rings*

DREAM OF YELLOW BLOSSOMS
Original size: 15.7 x 19.7 in

The ground material is dyed silk fabric stretched over a foam core board.
The *Chains of Josephine Rings* were placed onto the fabric without adhesive. The board and glass,
fixed in a frame, holds the work in place.

THE *PICOT RING*

A ring of continuous *PICOTS* (between *DOUBLE KNOTS*)
Application: for all sorts of flowers and leaves

CHAIN OF *PICOT RINGS*

Many *Picot Rings* worked
one after another
Application: for all sorts of foliage

BLOSSOM

From *Picot Rings* using variegated thread and flipped back *Picots (3-shuttle work)*

INSTRUCTIONS:

1. *Creative Knot.*
2. * red *Picot Ring.*
3. Flip *Picot Ring* backwards and use brown thread to make a *Reverse Knot* over the red and green threads.

4. Repeat from * six times.

5. Place brown thread between the first and second *Picot Ring* and slide the first and last *Picot Rings* on top of each other. Work another *Reverse Knot* with brown thread over red and green threads to close the round.

6. Gather all *Picot Rings* by pulling on the green thread, while arranging the blossom.

WORKING SUGGESTIONS AND APPLICATIONS

COMBINATIONS OF *JOSEPHINE-* AND *PICOT RINGS*

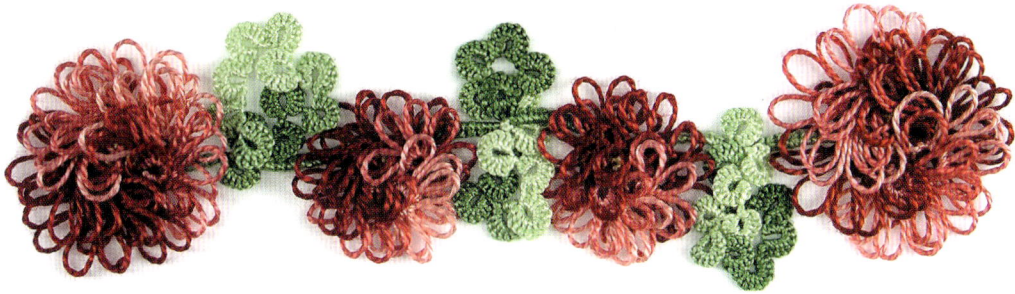

INSTRUCTIONS (3-shuttle work):

Work with variegated red, variegated green, and yellow (for the pistil) threads.

1. *Creative Knot.*
2. Blossom as described previously (seven rings with very long *Picots*).
3. Stem: Ten green *Reverse Knots* over red and yellow threads.
4. Leaf: *Chains of 12 Josephine Rings* with green thread, tied onto stem *(See pg. 14).*
5. Stem: Ten green *Reverse Knots.*
6. Smaller blossom with seven medium sized *Picots.*
7. Two leaves: two chains each with seven *Josephine Rings,* tied back as previously described.

Plants with *Josephine* and *Picot Rings (See pgs. 16 and 17),* using variegated thread. The bottom leaves consist of different sized *Picot Rings.*

The bottom leaves of the last plant are a *Chain of Picot Rings* with both small and very large *Picots.* All *Picot Rings* were glued onto the ground in an offset manner on top of each other.

23

PLANT VARIATIONS WITH *PICOT RINGS*
3-shuttle work with red, green and brown threads

PLANT 1

1. *Creative Knot* with red, green and brown threads.
2. *small *Picot Ring* in red.
3. A few green *Reverse Knots* over red and brown threads.
4. Repeat from * 5 times and add a few more green *Reverse Knots.*
5. Chain of small *Picot Rings*.
6. Tie onto stem with a few *Reverse Knots* over red and brown.
7. Work second *Chain of Picot Rings*.
8. Again, tie with *Reverse Knot* over red and brown.
9. Work stem and blossoms as before but shorten the space between the blooms.
10. Work a split *Creative Knot* and cut threads short.

PLANT 2

Small *Picot Rings* form the tip of the left stalk, continuing with increasingly larger ones. Two *Picot Rings* are always knotted one right after the other and placed on the left and right sides of the stem. The right stalk carries only small *Picot Rings*, but these too are worked in pairs, which are placed on either side of the stem. The left ground leaves are large *Picot Rings*, worked as a *Chain* and knotted back onto the stem, whereas the ground leaves on the right end are a *Chain* of increasingly smaller *Picot Rings*. With a *Reverse Knot* over the red and brown pull-thread, the green thread was added again to work the second stem.

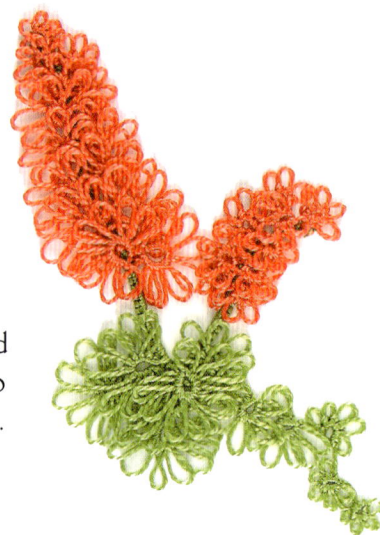

PLANT 3

Here, not just two, but three small *Picot Rings* or *Josephine Rings* were worked closely together with the third *Ring* always flipped back onto the other two.

The ground leaves are two ending *Chains of Picot Rings*, with thread ends cut short and incorporated again with a *Reverse Knot* over red and brown threads.

COMBINATIONS OF *PICOT* AND *JOSEPHINE RINGS* IN PLANT FORMS
3-shuttle work

PLANT 1
1. *Creative Knot* with all three colors.
2. * red *Josephine Ring* and small green *Picot Ring* worked in sequence and tied to the stem with green *Reverse Knots* over red and brown threads for the stem. Repeat continuously from *.

PLANT 2
1. *Creative Knot* with all three colors.
2. * *Picot Ring* with red thread.
3. Two green *Josephine Rings* worked close to each other and tied together with green *Reverse Knots* over red and brown threads.
4. A few more green *Reverse Knots*. Repeat continuously from *.

PLANT 3
1. *Creative Knot* with all three colors.
2. * medium sized green *Picot Ring* and three red *Josephine Rings* worked in sequence and tied together with brown *Reverse Knots* over red and green threads. Repeat continuously from *.

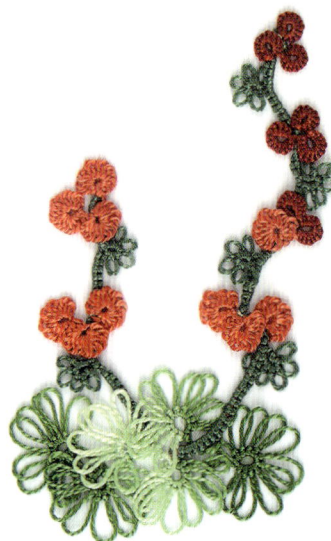

For both of these plants the dark green thread makes the stems and the stem leaves.
Both the red and the other green thread are carried inside the stems. The ground leaves are *Chains of Picot Rings,* which again are tied back to the stem.

The red thread is hidden in the
left stem

Third thread is brown pull-thread
inside each stem

INSTRUCTIONS:

Three flower stalks: Short left branch with one blossom, right branch with three blossoms, center branch with three blossoms and four leaves.

The two smaller branches, left and right, were knotted separately and combined with the main stem while pasting. The ground leaves consist of a *Chain* of *Picot Rings* made with large picots, which were assembled at time of pasting. The four bunches of grass belong to a hidden *Picot Ring* with two very large *Picots*, which were cut open after pasting and the tips frayed with a needle.

INSTRUCTIONS:

This plant was pasted together from many separate parts: One long stem with three blossoms and two leaves, four blossoms with small stems and two *Chains of Picot Rings* for the ground foliage.

The grass consists of two very large *Picots* each that were cut open and the ends frayed with a needle.

SUGGESTION
One can knot a variety of separate pieces and later arrange them while pasting them onto a ground material.

27

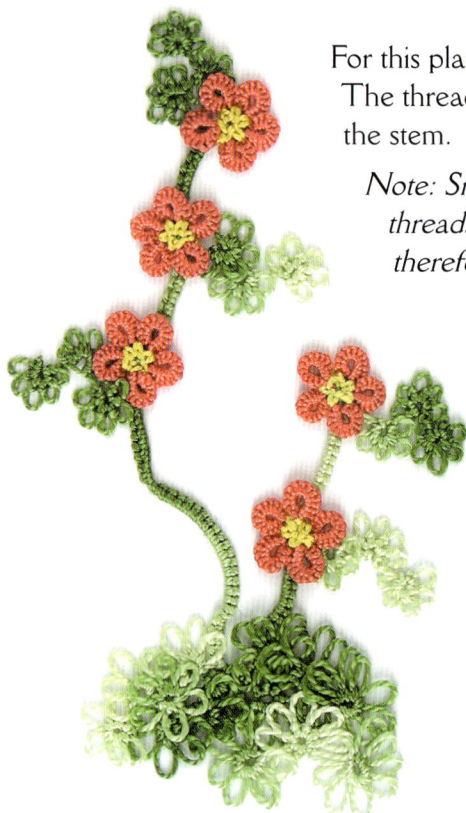

For this plant all of the stem leaves consist of three adjacent *Picot Rings*. The thread is always cut short and then incorporated again to continue the stem.

Note: Since the Reverse Knots for the stem work over the other two threads, they will be pushed together tightly, securing all threads. It is therefore not necessary to add the thread with a Creative Knot.

The ground leaves are a *Chain of Picot Rings,* added in final assembly by pasting.

This plant was worked in three segments:

1. Center part with two blossoms (top and bottom) and three leaves (double and triple *Picot Rings*).

2. Three separate blossom/stem elements (one left, two right).

3. Ground leaves from two *Chains of Picot Rings* (one directly attached, the other added while pasting).

All flowering branches were worked with 3 shuttles.
The start is always a *Creative Knot* and the end is
always a S*plit Creative Knot*.

To paste onto a ground, lay the separate
pieces down, lift them at the tip with
forceps and apply glue to the underside with
the tip of a knife, awl or needle being careful
that the glue does not draw threads. Now
press the branch sections, piece by piece onto
the paper.

Branch from *Josephine Rings* and *Shells* on a cotton t-shirt.

Thread: #8 perle cotton

Tendril and separate blossoms from *Josephine Rings* and leaves from *Chains of Josephine Rings*. Knotted as a tendril and as single elements.

Ironed onto a dress of raw silk.

Thread: #8 perle cotton

Tendril and single blossom/leaf elements on a t-shirt. Blossoms are *Josephine Rings* and leaves are *Chains of Josephine Rings*.

Thread: Metallic threads, black for the blossoms, silver for the pistils. Leaves are variegated green lace thread combined with metal filament, wound together onto one shuttle.

This is a four-part tendril with leaves of *Gathered Chains of Josephine Rings.* Assembly of the four parts done while ironing them onto front and back of the t-shirt.

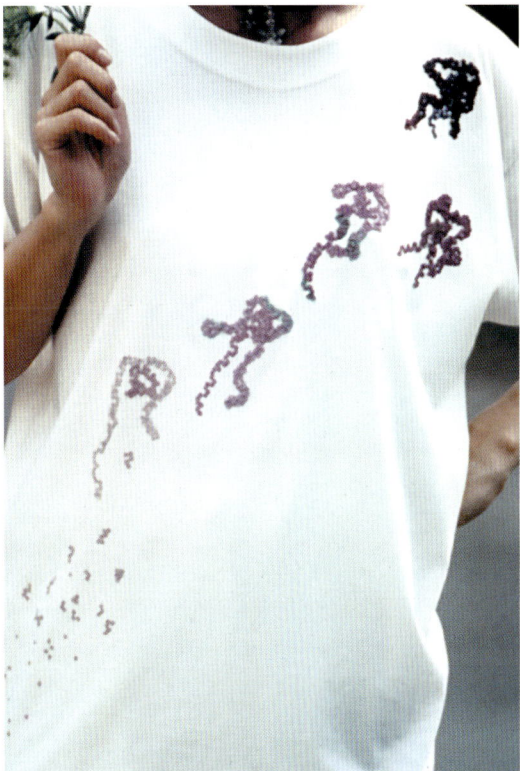

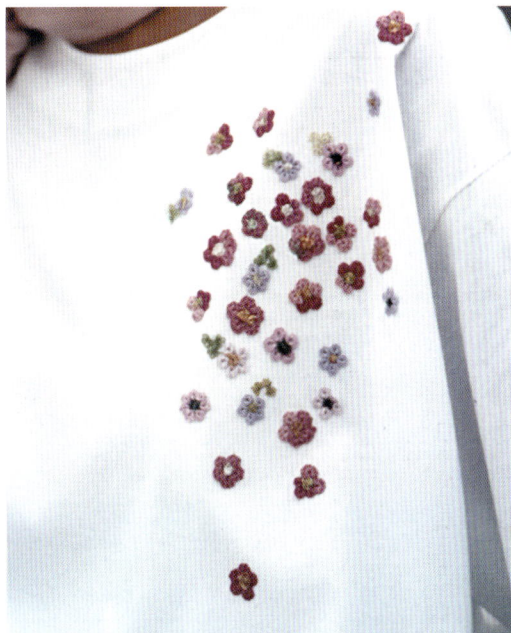

Two very casually composed motifs: *Left:* Five *Chains of Josephine Rings,* which were simply dropped onto the ironing board before adding the adhesive, accepting their random distribution; on the bottom many small parts of a *Chain of Josephine Rings. Right:* Individual small flowers placed randomly onto a t-shirt.

This tendril was worked with three shuttles even though it has four colors. The blossom/bud branches use two colors only (dark pink/medium pink or medium pink/dark pink) plus the green thread. For each start of a new blossom/bud branch one thread is cut off and a new one added by means of a *Creative Knot*.

All *Josephine Rings* were worked in dark pink, *Shells* in medium pink and *Picot Rings* in light pink.

The leaves are *Chains of Josephine Rings* tied back to the branch.

Hint: This tendril can also be worked in pieces and ironed together onto the fabric.

This center cloth has eight tendrils, pairs positioned in mirror image. You can also use just six of the tendrils in sequence.

This tendril is worked in four colors with three shuttles. Begin at the tip (left) with one beige and one white *Chain of Josephine Rings*. Light green thread is added with a *Creative Knot*, the tendrils then tied together while working the stems. White thread is used for the next *Chain of Josephine Rings*. The thread is cut off short and added again with a *Creative Knot*. The same is true for the beige *Chain of Josephine Rings*. The work is continued in this manner with subsequent color switches for the leaves.

The flowers were worked separately with three shuttles using variegated pink thread and added at the time of application onto the fabric.

This pattern can also be used as an applique on such wearables as a t-shirt, a dress, a blouse, or the waistband of a skirt.

Tip: All thread ends can be cut short as the iron-on adhesive will secure them.

Part of a table
center cloth
with purple
flowers.

A basic design
suitable
for many
variations.

VARIATIONS

1. Begin the large center plant with the light part of the variegated purple thread at the tip and end with the dark part. To do this, exchange the knotted elements: tip: *Josephine Rings*; bottom: *Picot Rings.*

2. Work the smaller plants left and right of the large one in the same fashion.

3. Switch the colors, that is, use light variegated purple for the large plant and darker variegated purple for the small plants.

4. Work the blossoms of the small plants on the left and right in *Josephine Rings* (as shown on p. 10).

Hint: The ground leaves are all chains: for the small plants Picot Rings, *for the large ones* Josephine Rings.
They can be added immediately by cutting off the purple blossom thread and adding a second green thread by means of a Creative Knot, *then finish off by making a complementary chain with both green threads.*

LITTLE FLOWERS ON A TABLECLOTH
3-shuttle work

Damask cloth with silk floss tatted flowers.

Petals: *Josephine Rings,* some with and some without *Picots.*

Green leaves: *Picot Rings*

Small flowers using #8 perle cotton on a cotton tablecloth, all worked in two colors and arranged randomly on the cloth after adding adhesive, and then fixing by ironing.

Petals: *Josephine Rings.*

Leaves: *Picot Rings.*

The semi-circles are worked in one piece as a tendril.

The flower circles consist of separate leaf-blossom-leaf motifs, which are ironed-on in a circular shape.

These models again demonstrate *Josephine Ring* blossoms and *Picot Ring* leaves, but this time with planned placment instead of random application.

Thread: #8 perle cotton.

The blossoms are *Josephine Rings* and the leaves small *Picot Rings* as in the previous example. The tendril however is worked as one continuous piece. Pink and white blossoms were mixed at random.

Elements in this sample each start with a *Chain of Josephine Rings*. After the first *Josephine Ring,* a pink thread is added for the blossom as well as a third thread with a *Creative Knot.* The third thread is not visible, its function only to pull the flower closed. Following the finished flower there is a second small *Chain of Josephine Rings.*

Hint: The last Josephine Ring *has to be pulled rather tightly so that it doesn't open up before being fixed with adhesive ironing.*

Placemat with a variegated purple *Picot Ring* border;
two tatted greeting cards; a potpourri bag; two bookmarks

Brooch, covered in silk with a *Josephine
Ring* blossom/leaf circle glued on.

Threads:

    Blossom petals: Lace thread wound together
        with metal filament.

    Pistils: 3-ply metallic thread.

    Leaves: #8 perle cotton.

POND

Original size: 15.7" x 19.7"
Ground material: art board
Knotted elements glued with aid of forceps
Thread: lace thread

The separate knotted elements were attached to art board with a glue stick using forceps.

The meadow background consists of *Chains of Picot Rings*. The clumps of grass are large cut *Picots* from several *Picot Rings*.

There are separately worked white, yellow, blue and purple larger flowers from *Chains of Josephine Rings* and single *Josephine Rings* for tiny flowers. These were glued onto a background of *Chains of Picot Rings*.

In the center of the pond one can make out "water lilies" consisting of two *Picot Rings*, a small yellow one glued on top of a larger white one.

1. *Picot Rings,* worked as *Chains,* form the background.
2. The purple plants, worked according to instructions on pg. 17.
3. Yellow *Josephine Rings,* in single, double or triple format.
4. Left: large, cut *picots* of *Picot Rings* form the grasses.

Example 1

The following pictures were put together with the same general methods as the previous one: "Heathland", "River Landscape" and "Summer Landscape". "Summer Landscape" has its elements fixed only by glass and frame while the other two have the separate motifs glued onto the art board with the help of forceps.

Example 2

For another background, *Chains of Josephine Rings* in various green shades with blossoms of *Josephine Rings* placed on top.

41

HEATHLAND

Original size: 15.7" x 19.7"
Ground material: art board
Knotted elements applied with aid of forceps
Thread: Lace thread

The juniper bush is made from separate green *Picot Rings*. All other plants are made from long *chains.* The far background consists of *Chains of Picot Rings* in light variegated thread, the *Picot Ring Chain* background in more intense variegated greens, and the flowering heath from short *Chains of Josephine Rings* in variegated red and purple thread.

Glue on dark brown *Picot Rings* with the longer *Picots* first. These are cut open before gluing. Then glue the smaller green *Picot Rings,* squeezed together, on top.

RIVER LANDSCAPE

Original size: 15.7" x 19.7"
Ground material: art board
Knotted elements applied with aid of forceps
Thread: Lace thread

In this picture the general landscape was first defined with *Chains of Picot Rings*. The background uses lighter variegated thread, the foreground uses darker thread to create depth. The clumps of grass are some very large, cut-open, *Picots* of *Picot Rings*. The white and variegated yellow blossom arrangements were worked as *Chains of Josephine Rings* and placed onto the *Chains of Picot Rings*. The blue plants of the foreground were knotted separately and incorporated into the picture during the final assembly.

SUMMER LANDSCAPE

Original size: 15.7" x 19.7"
Ground material: painted silk
Knotted elements placed loosely onto ground and held by glass and frame
Thread: Lace thread in background and #8 perle cotton foreground

The mature cornfield is created by *Chains of Picot Rings*. The *Picots* were cut open after slight attachment of the chain on each end, the following chains attached densely in the same manner.

The cornfield is bordered by a green stripe of *Chains of Picot Rings* from variegated green, arranged loosely. The left corner bears solid green *Chains of Picot Rings*, which have single *Josephine Rings*, knotted as a chain and then separated, applied on top.

The clumps of grass are cut-open *Picot Rings* applied individually. The whole splendor of blossoms on the small hill are *Chains of Josephine Rings*, applied onto *Chains of Picot Rings*, using different sizes of thread.

NEW IDEAS IN TATTING
PART II
WORKING WITH *CATWALK PICOTS*

CATWALK PICOTS

A chain of alternating *Reverse Knots* and *Reverse Picots* forms the *Catwalk Picot.* The thread on the left hand is the core thread and the right one is the working thread, that is, it will be used up.

1. One *Catwalk* with many *Reverse Picots* of same size.
   (brown: core thread; green: working thread)

2. Initially increasing, then decreasing sizes of *Catwalk Picots* to form an angular shape .
   (brown: core thread; green: working thread)

3. The size of the *Picots* can be changed at will, that is, it can constantly change according to your imagination of a natural form.

4. A *Catwalk* that has been twisted once (here green is the core thread and brown is the working thread).

   Start with a few brown *Reverse Knots*; follow with a section of a few normal-size *Picots*, then a few increasingly larger *Picots*.

   At some point twist the *Chain of Catwalk Picots*, so that a section of the *Picots* points up followed by another section pointing down.

5. This tapered chain of *Catwalk Picots* was twisted five times.

Hint: Begin and end your work with a Creative Knot.

COMPOSITION OF TREES WITH *CATWALK PICOTS*
2-shuttle work

This tree starts at the left root with a *Creative Knot*. Initially only *Reverse Knots* were worked and then large *Reverse Picots* to form the trunk. For the branches the *Reverse Picots* become smaller again, finishing up with *Reverse Knots* only. Some thread ends were left to depict roots or thin branches.

The right side of the tree was worked similarly. Two more separately worked branches complete the treetop which can progressively be filled with foliage of *Chains of Josephine* or *Picot Rings. (See p. 48 top).*

TWIRLED *CATWALK PICOTS*

For twirling, grab both left and right thread ends and twist (twirl) them between thumb and forefinger so that the picots come to lie pointing upwards and downwards.

To form a branch, always begin with a *Creative Knot,* work a row of green over brown *Reverse Picots,* switch shuttles, and continue to knot the branch with brown *Reverse Knots* or *Reverse Picots.* Finish with a *Split Creative Knot.*

Hint: Using variegated threads for the foliage will give the impression of light and shadow.

A TREE DESIGN

This tree is composed of twirled branches, as described on the previous page, the elements glued in place. More branches, of course, could be added.

In this case the trunk has a rough bark (in contrast to the previous example). This was achieved by placing the two *Catwalk Picot Chains with* picots facing away from each other, the knotted edges in the center, in contrast to the example on page 47. The trunk center has the dense edges, the outside has the picot tips.

For fuller, more luscious foliage, one can add previously worked, twisted *Catwalk Picots* to the branches with the *Thread Scissors* technique *(See pg. 7).*

Other types of chains can be added with the *Thread Scissors* technique to give the foliage completely different appearances. For instance chains of:

Josephine Rings (See pg. 13)   *Shells (See pg. 15)*   *Picot Rings (See pg. 22)*

Begin at the tip of a branch, first making a chain (here a *Chain of Picot Rings*). Add a brown thread (with reverse knots) to build the branch. Then you can continuously add previously worked chains using the *Thread Scissors.*

The SUMMER POPLAR was worked in the following manner:

The top starts with a *Chain of Josephine Rings.* This was followed by two or three brown *Reverse Knots* formed over the green thread. *Josephine Ring Chains* were then added in continuous fashion, each secured with *Thread Scissors* and separated by two to five brown *Reverse Knots.*

The ground foliage at the base of the trunk is a *Chain of Picot Rings* with a mixture of small *Picots* and large cut *Picots. This was* worked separately and added after placement of the tree on the painted silk ground.

SUMMER POPLAR

This windswept FALL POPLAR, which was tatted following the same principles as the previous tree, shows how the work can be shaped during arrangement of the elements onto the ground fabric of painted silk.

Elements of both trees are held in place by glass and frame.

FALL POPLAR

49

WORKING OPTIONS

From left to right on the branch
illustrated:

Start: *Creative Knot*

a. Branch from very small brown *Reverse Picots* over green, twisted once.

b. Small leaves: one small *Picot Ring*.

c. Twisted branch: *Reverse Knots*.

d. Small leaves: two small *Picot Rings*, tied together with the first brown *Reverse Knot* over green.

e. Branch: as before.

f. Small leaves: three small *Picot Rings* tied together as before.

g. Branch, not twisted.

h. Leaf: *Chain of Picot Rings* (thread was cut off short at the end and added again with brown using a *Creative Knot* - see green thread).

i. Longer branch: not twisted but a bit thicker in appearance due to *Reverse Picots*.

j. Leaf: *Chain of Picot Rings* tied up. Simply return the green thread to the beginning of the chain and continue knotting over it with brown thread *(See pg. 14)*.

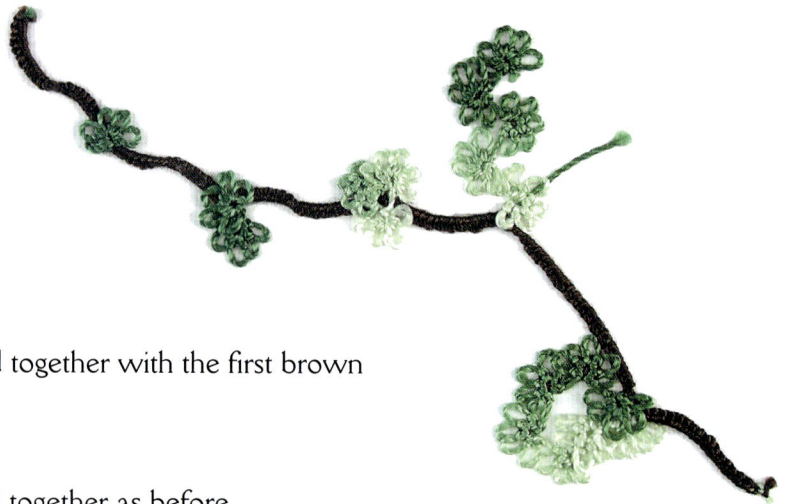

This picture clearly illustrates the technique of tying up chains, here, *Chains of Josephine Rings*.

The back and forth twists of the *Catwalk Picots* nicely accentuate the gnarled appearance of the trunks.

This tree was tatted according to the working principles *h.* and *j.* on previous page.

The left half of the tree was made in a delicate fashion with thinner branches and using only the lighter parts of the variegated green thread.

The background is painted silk fabric.

This tree was worked in the same manner, but more exuberantly and hence stronger in appearance. Observe also how the final design shape depends on the arrangement of the elements on the silk background.

In this work too, fixing the placement of the tatting elements with glass and frame gives the complete picture a rather lively appearance.

Note: Holding the picture together with glass and frame allows you to simply place the knotted elements loosely onto the background, which always produces a more natural effect than elements that are secured by glue.

51

This birch tree follows principle *h.* described on pg. 50, clearly recognizable on the left lower branch.

There are a total of five such branches. To show a dying branch, one was knotted using a brown variegated thread instead of the green variegated thread.

The trunk is composed of three *Chains of Catwalk Picots,* knotted in two different variegated browns.

Background material is art board. Attachment was done with forceps and a glue stick.

The more experienced tatter, observing nature closely, will note that the birch trunk can be made much more lifelike by intentionally switching shuttles to pick the light or dark values of the variegated threads.

BLOOMING CHERRY TREE

After securing the tree skeleton *(See pg. 47),* several groups of small and large *Picot Rings*, three to five knots each, were added separately.

Background: art board.
Thread: lace weight.

FALL POPLAR IN A STORM

Here the foliage consists of separately knotted elements: Single *Picot Rings* that each have small, as well as large, picots. These were arranged to depict wind direction during assembly with forceps and glue stick with the larger *Picots* cut open afterwards.

Background: art board.
Thread: lace weight.

Evergreen Trees
2 shuttle work

Begin with a *Creative Knot*. Knot the crown with green over brown, working short *Catwalk Picots tapering* from small to large *Reverse Picots*. Twist this top once when gluing. Now switch shuttles and knot the trunk, with brown over green, with increasingly larger *Reverse Picots*. Finish with a *Split Creative Knot*.

Make the branches from separate *Chains of Catwalk Picots* with the *Picots* of varying sizes. Finally, arrange everything and glue in place.

Nature does not contain only beautifully formed trees. As shown here, one can also work crippled pines and gnarled firs in creative tatting.

The trunk of this pine, for instance, is a *Chain of Catwalk Picots* that has been twisted six times.

Background material is painted silk.

A CHRISTMAS TREE

See following pages for instructions on working the separate branches and their ornaments.

Following the *Creative Knot* in green, red and gold:

First work green *Catwalk Picots* over red and gold.

To form the first half of the candle, work a *Chain* of red *Reverse Knots* over gold. The flame is a golden *Ring*, which, in this case, consists of a single *Double Knot*, a very large *Picot* and a second *Double Knot*.

Now work the same in reverse:

To keep the candle straight, work the second half of the candle with the same number of *Reverse Knots* as the first half.

The two candle halves are tied together with a green *Reverse Knot* over the red and gold thread.

Knot the other half of the green branch and finish off with a *Split Creative Knot.*

The gold thread can also be used, while knotting the branch with green over red and gold, to add embellishments as shown in the following examples. See additional examples on next page.

This example shows the gold thread used to work three consecutive *Josephine Rings* while working the *Reverse Picots* for the green branch. When continuing with green the *Josephine Rings* get tied together.

Instead of just three *Josephine Rings* (see above) this example shows a *Chain of Josephine Rings.* Drop the entire chain including the shuttle and continue with a few more green *Reverse Picots,* over only the red thread, then take the gold and red threads and tat green *Reverse Picots over them.*

This branch was worked in the same way, but with the decorative chain consisting of a *Chain of Picot Rings* instead of *Josephine Rings.*

For the gold spray, a bunch of metallic threads was laid over the two core threads of red and gold between the green *Reverse Knots.* Continue knotting. The *Josephine Ring* on the right side was added after a short distance and then the gold thread added to the core again, knotted with green over red and gold.

This candle was not worked as before in *Reverse Knots,* but from *Reverse Picots* and then placed onto a separately knotted branch that was twisted twice. The flame was worked with doubled metallic thread in the following sequence: four picots, small to large, and then four more picots, large to small.

57

CATWALK PICOT FLOWERS
2-shuttle work

Creative Knot, red over green *Reverse Picots,* then switch shuttles for green over red *Reverse Knots.*

Make a spiral from the *Catwalk Picot Chain* to form the blossom and glue.

GROUND LEAVES MADE FROM CATWALK PICOTS

Creative Knot with 3 threads.
Blossom: *Shells* for the flower petals and
Reverse Knot to form the pistil (blossoms, *See pg. 10*).
Stem: *Reverse Knots* over two threads.
Ground Leaves: green *Catwalk Picots* over yellow thread, setting the blue thread aside, into the left hand.

Now work a green *Reverse Knot* over blue and yellow to close the circle. With this you are tying three threads together.

Switch the blue and yellow threads, putting the yellow one out of the way, over the left hand. Make *Reverse Picots* in green over blue and again tie both threads together with a *Reverse Knot.*

After this work the second stem and flower to complete the plant *(See pg. 9).* Finish in typical fashion with a *Split Creative Knot.*

MORE EXAMPLES OF LEAVES MADE FROM *CATWALK PICOTS*

In the example on the previous page, the ground leaves were *Reverse Picots* of irregular sizes. To generate more defined shapes, work evenly sized picots and shift them together before gluing the work down so that the knotted sides of the *Catwalk Picot Chains* face each other, giving the leaf a defined center rib.

To make a leaf with a narrow tip, uniformly decrease *Picot* size to the center, and then increase *Picot* size going back.

Continue as shown on the previous page: tie all threads together with a green *Reverse Knot* over the other two threads, here red and yellow.

When making two or, as here, three leaves one after each other, one can continue with a second stem and flower *(See pg 9)*.

Obviously, you can continue this exercise to form a tendril.

OTHER SUGGESTIONS

1. Make larger or smaller leaves. In this case there are ten picots on each side of the rib.
2. Work irregular distances between leaves and flowers of the tendril.
3. Don't always place leaves and flowers in a regular fashion, in other words, put two or three flowers together and vary the sequence and number of flowers and leaves.
4. Use threads of different thicknesses for leaves and flowers. This example uses #8 perle cotton.

The bottom left leaf consists of 25 *Picots* of the same size, the right one has 50.
The upper section of the right leaf was folded over and glued.

In this example both ground leaves are the same size. The left one was twisted twice and, in contrast to the previous plant, the bottom half of the chain was folded upwards.

There are four variations used in these ground leaves:
1. The left one was tatted entirely in a zig-zag shape.
2. Only the lower half of the right one is sig-zag.
3. All picots of the upper half are the same size.
4. Both *Catwalk Picot Chains* were pushed together, compressing them for gluing.

There are four variations used in this plant:
1. All picots are of the same size in each leaf.
2. Leaves differ in picot length.
3. There are three ground leaves, all worked one after the other.
4. The flowers show their pistils, which are made up of brown *Reverse Picots* rather than *Reverse Knots*.

ANOTHER SUGGESTION

Work large and small ground leaves for a plant and separate them, after finishing a leaf, with two to three green *Reverse Knots* over the other two threads.

BELLFLOWER FROM *CATWALK PICOTS*
3-SHUTTLE WORK

Start with a *Creative Knot,* drop brown shuttle, take
the green thread onto the left hand and work five
green *Picots* with yellow shuttle. Note: these are regular
Double Knots and *Picots* as shown on pg. 8, not *Reverse
Picots.* Continue with seven yellow *Reverse Picots.*

Now bend the yellow *Catwalk Picots* downward, tie the
green and yellow threads together with the brown thread.

Now you could
continue, making a small plant...

...or, repeat this process a few
times for a larger one.

This plant was worked in the same way. The third
thread, however, runs inside the stems and only appears
with the ground leaves as a different green.

The blossoms were made from lace thread, and
both greens are #8 perle cotton.

The following pictures were all tatted from the examples shown on the previous page.

Thread: lace
Background: art board
Assembly: glue stick and forceps.

Six separately knotted, different plants.

Seven separate plants assembled into one.

Floral grouping worked in the *Catwalk Picot* technique, shown near original size.

NEW IDEAS IN TATTING

PART III

WORKING WITH *OVER-CROCHETED PICOT RINGS*

HERBACEOUS PLANT
(details on pg 71)

THE COMPLEX ROUND KNOTTING ELEMENTS

THE *OVER-CROCHETED PICOT RING* FLOWER *(3-shuttle work)*

Following a *Creative Knot*, work a *Picot Ring*.

With one of the three threads, here light pink, crochet a chain up to the height of the last picot...

...then over-crochet the ring from picot to picot, here with single crochet, and finally some additional chain stitches to return to starting point.

Pull the crochet thread through the center of the *Picot Ring* and put the shuttle through the loop to lock.

After closing the loop, work the first *Reverse Picot* for the pistil over the other two threads.

Repeat these five steps four times, lay the thread used for the pistil over the first petal worked...

...and knot another *Reverse Knot* behind it over the other two threads to close the circle of petals.

The finished blossom.

65

Flower Variations

This blossom has five petals knotted from variegated thread. This has the advantage that the third thread, here green, will not be used for knotting. Pulling on this thread at the end will draw all petals into a denser petal round, enabling you to control the blossom shape.

Green thread covers red and brown threads to work the stem.

This blossom was worked with variegated thread and has six petals...

...this one has seven petals. It is possible to make even more which would overlap, as would be desirable if making a rose.

There are many variations for *Over-Crocheting*:

The flower on the left was tatted in dark red and *Over-Crocheted* with light red. the flower on the right has the colors reversed.

For these flowers the picots were worked in different sizes so that the *Over-Crocheting* in the contrast yarn had to incorporate double crochet stitches to even out the petals.

66

A flower with two large petals and three smaller ones,

This one has three large ones and two smaller ones.

For this flower the petals were worked with a tapered shape just like the candle flame on *pg. 57*. For compensation, work two to three chain stitches between the single crochets when *Over-Crocheting* the picots.

This blossom is a combination of the first and third flower.

Here, the first and last three picots are large and the three center ones small. Note that the *Over-Crochet* incorporates some chain stitch compensation.

A completely different edge is created by *Over-Crocheting* the picots with a zig-zag crochet, made by crocheting a picot at the tip of each tatted picot.

THE *OVER-CROCHETED PICOT RING* FOR LEAVES

Chain of several *Over-Crocheted Picot Rings* of the same size using a single shuttle.

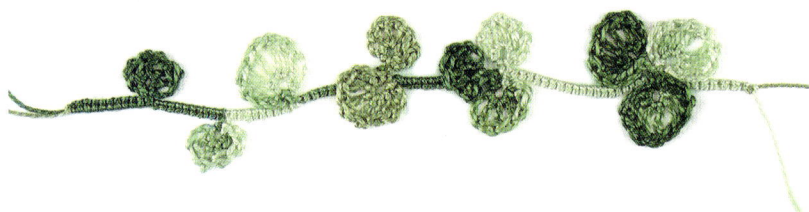

For this tendril of leaves two shuttles were used to create the thicker stem. Groups of two and three *Over-Crocheted Picot Rings* were tied together with the next *Reverse Knot*.

A *Chain* of small *Over-Crocheted Picot Rings* worked with one shuttle, with the simple addition of a second thread at the end to form a thicker stem with *Reverse Knots*.

This tendril of leaves was worked just like the previous one but the single *Over-Crocheted Picot Rings* were set closer to each other.

There are many possibilities for further variations. Here for instance is a very large *Picot Ring*, which had to be over-crocheted with not just double crochet but treble crochet, and larger stitches to compensate for different picot sizes.

Here too, another possible way to over-crochet the picots is the zig-zag form, incorporating picots in the crochet *(see pg 67)*.

OTHER SUGGESTIONS

1. Crochet into two picots at the same time.

2. Make the last picot of the ring very small and first work a crochet chain up to the tip of the next picot creating a firm border.

To get a whole pile of leaves, as for the ground leaves of this plant, one can tie together the beginning and the end of the chain with *Reverse Knots* over the other two threads, as shown here with the ground leaves.

Procedure:
Creative Knot; blossom; stem; ground leaves of a *Chain of Over-Crocheted Picot Rings,* gathered with *Reverse Knots* over the other two threads; stem; blossom; *Split Creative Knot.*

To depict a wilted flower one can use a brown variegated thread to over-crochet the *Picot Rings.*

One can add a lively character to blossoms as well. In this example the *Picot Rings* were tatted in large and small sizes and over-crocheted with a lighter or darker thread of the same shade, alternating single and double crochet stitches.

69

To create realistic plants, one has to closely observe nature. Blossoms don't always face you in an "open" manner, but are often turned away or twisted from wind or weather influence, or they appear lighter or darker due to varying light and shadows.

By combining large and small *Over-Crocheted Picot Rings* one can change the appearance of the point of view of the flower. Using lighter and darker shades of the same color will generate light and shadow effects.

This example gains reality by using light and dark purple thread, for knotting as well as crochet.

Here we easily recognize the pansy, as well as the working sequence using material from the previous lessons. The pistil was made from very large *Reverse Picots.*

SUGGESTION

The fourth thread, here always green, can be added after finishing the blossom and tatting over the other three threads with *Reverse Knots,* and then cutting the beginning thread short after a few knots. If necessary, two threads can be cut off after the blossom is done. The third thread is enough to make the stem, working *Reverse Knots* over it.

HERBACEOUS PLANT
(also shown on page 64)

After a *Creative Knot* of variegated red, variegated green and dark brown thread, make the large branch with the three blossoms and leaves. The ground leaves are a *Chain* of seven small *Over-Crocheted Picot Rings*. Drop the red and brown threads here. This chain is tied back onto itself with *Reverse Knots* over the red and brown thread. This is followed by the second chain of leaves, this time from seven larger *Over-Crocheted Picot Rings*, and again, tied back onto itself. The second bunch of flowers is worked with the larger one on the bottom and the smaller one above it. Everything is completed with a *Split Creative Knot*. The small blossom on the left is worked separately and added later.

In making this picture, the green shuttle emptied twice and new thread had to be added with a *Creative Knot*. There were four thread ends, two ending and two beginning, that were left rather long. Their tips were frayed with the point of a needle after gluing them in place.

The flower petals as well as the green leaves are all of the same size *Over-Crocheted Picot Rings* of five small picots. The brown and red threads were cut short after each blossom and the leaves were continued in green. The green thread was then cut off short.

For this design all petals are a bit larger, using seven picots, with the green leaves arranged towards the center. As above, this design consists of three separately worked blossoms and leaves.

These blossoms consist of even larger *Over-Crocheted Picot Rings*. The leaves are chains of small *Picot Rings*.

All were worked with variegated thread.

In this piece, the tendril image is shown again. It is worked all in one piece. For each color change from larger to smaller blossoms, and vice versa, a new variegated red thread is added with a *Creative Knot* and the previous one cut short. The same holds true for the tendril of leaves to the left. After the last *Over-Crocheted Picot Ring*, the thread is cut off short and then used for the *Reverse Knots* of the stems.

72

Working with three shuttles, the blossoms are tatted separately using white, purple and yellow threads. The white thread is used alternating with the purple variegated thread, sometimes for knotting and other times for crochet.

The leaf tendrils use two shuttles with two different green threads for both knots and crochet.

The composition of the blossoms and the color distribution for the leaves is identical to the example above.

The leaf tendrils use two shuttles and formed with zig-zag form *Over-Crocheted Picot Rings (See pg 67)*.

SUGGESTIONS

1. Work the blossoms with a darker shade of the same color instead of white.
2. Work the leaf tendrils with green and brown threads to form stems.
3. *Over-Crochet* some of the leaves with brown to depict wilting.

These blossoms were worked as *Over-Crocheted Picot Rings* (see *pg. 66*).

For the tendril of leaves, the shuttles with the lighter and darker thread were switched every so often.

A mix of shapes, colors and several knotting elements.

Flowers:
Refer to pgs. 10, 22, 65, 66, 67

(See Part V for instructions for the two pink blossoms at the bottom)

Tendrils:
1. *Chain of Picot Rings:* lower left. *(See pg. 22).* Groups of three picot rings are worked close together and spaced a short distance from the next group.

2. *Chain of Josephine Rings:* right center *(See pg. 13).*

3. Gathered *Chains of Josephine Rings* (See pg. 14).

4. *Over-Crocheted Picot Rings* (See pg. 65).

HINT

To glue, lift the tatted element up a little with forceps and dab some glue to the backside with the tip of a knife or pin. Then simply press the tatted element onto the ground fabric.

A simple tendril with small white blossoms from *Josephine Rings,* light red flowers of *Over-Crocheted Picot Rings* and dark red ones made from overlapping *Picot Rings.* The leaves are *Chains of Josephine Rings* and separate small *Picot Rings.*

A colorful table band for a child's birthday with constantly changing motifs and colors. To change the threads the new one is always added with a *Creative Knot* and the old one cut off short, after two to three *Reverse Knots* for the stem.

This band uses dark and light pink and two shades of green. To use the light green thread for the pistils, one has to switch shuttles to work the dark green *Chains of Josephine Rings, i.e.,* the new thread is added with a *Creative Knot* and the old one cut off short after two to three *Reverse Knots,* for the stem.

The tendril gets its liveliness with the undulating path, the ever-changing arrangement of the *Chains of Josephine Rings,* and the different color distribution for each blossom.

For this square tablecloth a tendril was ironed on along the seams and a second one, slightly lighter in color and smaller in size, from edge center to center across the corners.

Corner detail

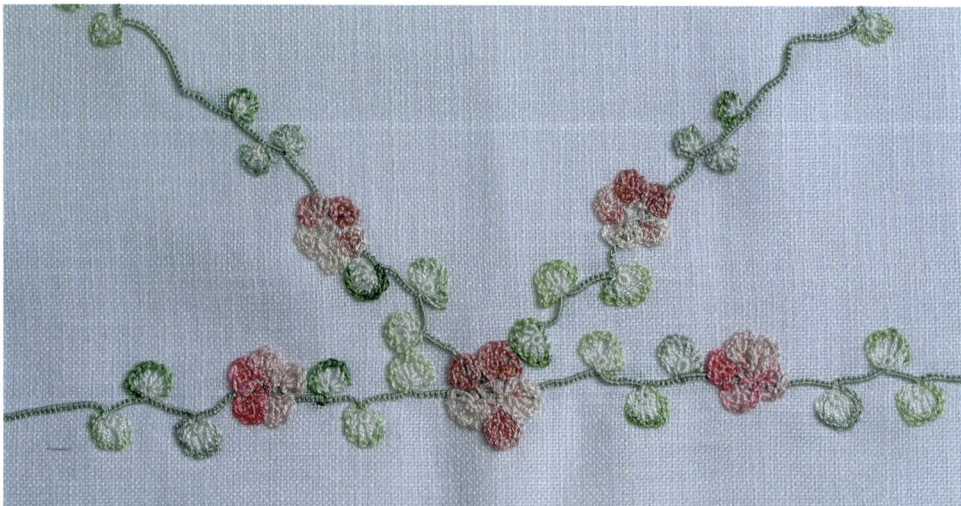

Side center detail

This tatting was done in variegated green, white and yellow. The white *Picot Rings* were *Over-Crocheted* in green. The corners consist of larger leaves that taper off to smaller ones towards the center of the cloth with ever increasing space between *Picot Rings.*

The yellow flower clusters are *Chains of Josephine Rings.* Threads were always cut off short and added again with a *Creative Knot.*

The corner

77

This corner motif consists of three separately knotted blossoms and four separately worked tendrils.

The side motif

The top blossom is five *Over-Crocheted Picot Rings,* the center seven and the bottom with ten.

Reverse Knots were used to make the pistils.

Progressing from top to bottom: a *Chain of Josephine Rings,* with two more added to the top blossoms.

In the corner of the tablecloth two tendrils of *Over-Crocheted Picot Rings* of ten, seven and five count meet, and taper off in a *Chain of Josephine Rings.*

78

This corner motif is similar to the previous one. It consists of three blossoms, a stem with two leaves and eight chains of *Josephine Rings,* two dark ones and two light ones on each side.

There are two smaller plants on the long sides and a medium sized one in the center that were worked in a similar manner.

On this tablecloth there are four tendrils that each begin in the center with a large blossom and end in the corners with a cluster of leaves.

This tendril uses dark red, light red and variegated beige thread.

The variegated beige thread is used as the pull thread for forming the blossoms. For the stems, both red threads are the core and are knotted over with *Reverse Knots* using the beige thread.

The corner motif here consists of 2 x 2 white flowering branches bunched up together with a yellow flowering branch where all threads were knotted over in green.

Instructions for the yellow branch: *Chain of Josephine Rings*, add a green thread with *Creative Knot*, then tie in a second, previously worked *Chain of Josephine Rings* with the *Thread Scissors* and continue with *Reverse Picots* to form the stem. All leaves are *Over-Crocheted Picot Rings*.

In all this abundance of flowers, not a single blossom occurs twice. Even the green tendrils of leaves are different and arranged with variations. However, all adhere to the same dimensions.

All the same, it is a very harmonious design, unified by consistent colors of purple, variegated purple and white.

Good contrasts to the large blossoms of *Over-Crocheted Picot Rings* are the randomly added small white flowers of *Josephine Rings,* which have pistils of the variegated purple.

The tatted appliqués were made from 3-ply sewing thread which better suits the fine character of the damask tablecloth.

Only three different reds were used. Because this thread is very fine, three strands can be wound together on the shuttle, allowing the possibility of nine different shades of red.

Thus, the color graduation is very subtle, which complements the fine nature of the damask fabric.

The blossoms and blossom/leaf elements were knotted in exactly the same way but arranged differently in each of the four corners. For a symmetrical design, the tendrils of leaves were arranged identically.

83

The other three corners of the tablecloth from *pg 83*.

New Ideas in Tatting
Part IV
Working with the *Gathered Picot Ring*

Prior to closing the ring:

Make seven picots (this number works best). Refer to pg. 11 for using a gauge.

Form a loop by pulling the working thread through the picots with a crochet hook and...

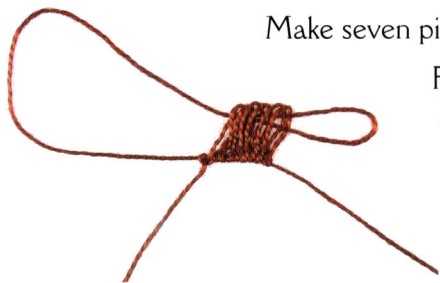

...put the shuttle through this loop and...

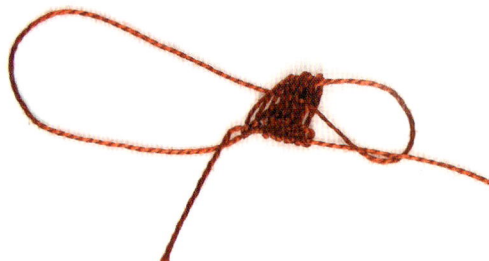

...loosely pull the loop closed.

Work one second half of a *Double Knot* (right knot) behind the picots.

Now tighten and pull the *Ring* closed.

If only some of the picots are gathered, here 4 of 7, the resulting element is called a *Partially Gathered Picot Ring*

VARIATIONS

1. Gather five or six of the seven picots.
2. Make the ungathered picots larger than the others.
3. Make the ungathered picots smaller than the others.
4. Cut the ungathered picots and fray their ends with the tip of a needle.

FLOWERS FROM GATHERED PICOT RINGS
3-shuttle work

After a *Creative Knot,* work the first petal with a *Gathered Picot Ring.*

Follow with a *Reverse Knot* over two threads.

Repeat this at least four more times

Now close the petal group, by working another *Reverse Knot* over the other two threads behind the first petal.

Finally, use the so-far unused third thread (core) to pull the petals together and tighten up the flower.

Now use the green thread to make the stem with *Reverse Knots* over red and brown, inserting a small leaf every so often.

With this technique one can make a tendril, as shown here, or a plant as on the bottom of the next page.

This blossom has five petals of *Completely Gathered Picot Rings* with seven picots each. Leaves on the stem are worked in the same way.

These blossoms have only three petals each and of the seven picots in the ring just six were gathered. Note that the three branches were tied together with *Reverse Knots* over all threads.

For this flower, a total of ten *Partially Gathered Picot Rings* were closed into a circle of petals. For each *Picot Ring* three picots were left ungathered. The green leaves are a chain of five *Gathered Picot Rings*. The pistil was worked in variegated brown *Reverse Knots*.

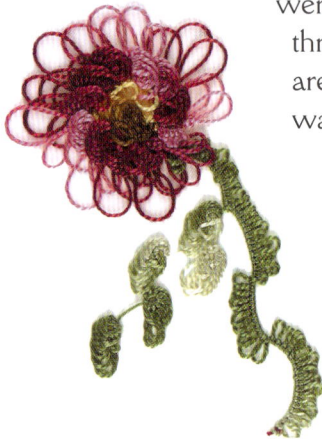

This branch was worked with three shuttles as well. The third thread runs with the pink variegated thread in the stem. Following a *Creative Knot*, a green *Completely Gathered Picot Ring* of seven *Picots was made* followed by two *Partially Gathered Picot Rings* in pink. This was repeated after a section of green stem.

The next two blossoms consist of three *Partially Gathered Picot Rings* adjacent to small green leaves.

These blossoms do not have a pistil, meaning that each *Gathered Picot Ring* is, by itself, a blossom.

Illustrating how one can arrange a flowering plant with blossoms from *Gathered Picot Rings*.

The *Gathered Picot Ring* - After - Closing the Ring
(Use of a picot gauge, preferably a larger one, is recommended.)

After the ring has been closed, pull the working thread through all the picots with a crochet hook.

Hold the picots tight, work two crochet chain stitches and lead the shuttle through the end loop...

.... and tighten the thread. Now lead the thread back down to the base of the ring and connect the thread again to the rest of the work with a *Split Creative Knot* over the other two threads *(See pg. 89 - 96).*

The *Gathered Picot Ring After Closing the Ring* is particularly well suited for large ground leaves.

Two Flowers Made with the *Gathered Picot Ring - After - Closing the Ring*
3-shuttle work

The petals as well as the ground leaves are made with *Gathered Picot Rings After Closing the Ring.*

INSTRUCTIONS (for the sunflowers shown on page 85 and at right using 1 and 2 shuttles):

The blossoms were worked in three steps and the leaves in two.

1. The pistils are *Chains of Josephine Rings.*

2. Around these are two rows of *Chains of Picot Rings* in variegated brown thread, followed by...

3. ...the circle of flower petals of *Gathered Picot Rings After Closing the Ring.* They were tatted in a row with two different yellow threads; each *Ring* separated by two to three *Reverse Knots.*

The green leaves are also *Gathered Picot Rings After Closing the Ring.* They were worked in two parts from two different green threads, with three *Reverse Knots* between the *Rings.*

The elements were glued to the ground fabric.

90

INSTRUCTIONS:

Creative Knot, Gathered Picot Ring bud, two to three brown *Reverse Knots* (over red and green), green *Josephine Ring,* etc. As you continue leave more and more *Picots* ungathered to imitate unfolding blossoms.

A chain of *Partially Gathered Picot Rings.* Use as all other chains for building foliage.

PLANT EXAMPLE

INSTRUCTIONS:

Creative Knot, Gathered Picot Ring, five brown *Reverse Knots* over red and green, small green *Picot Ring,* more stem work, next bud and so on.

At the end of stem: Chain of *Partially Gathered Picot Rings,* tied back to the stem with *Reverse Knots,* a second chain, again tied back, then a second stem with leaves from small *Picot Rings* and red elements from *Gathered Picot Rings, Split Creative Knot.* Cut all threads short.

In this example all knotted elements consist of *Gathered Picot Rings*.

All rings at the stem are gathered *before* closing and the three consecutively worked ground leaves are rings gathered *after* closing of the ring.

For this plant three *before* closing *Gathered Picot Rings* were separated with a brown *Reverse Knot* (over green and purple) in continuous fashion and tied together with a *Thread Scissors* to form a blossom. Leaves on the stem are small *Picot Rings*. The ground leaves consist of three *after* closing *Gathered Picot Rings*.

Here are five ground leaves, worked close together and tied to the first stem, and two *Josephine Rings* for each calyx.

The "grass" in these examples is made by adding a new thread and fraying the tips with a needle.

The blossoms are three *Partially Gathered Picot Rings*, each separated by a small brown *Reverse Picot* for the pistil, and tied together with a *Thread Scissors*. The leaves on the stem are three small consecutively knotted *Gathered Picot Rings*. For this small size, a picot gauge is not necessary. The largest ground leaf was twisted once before gluing for a little more interest.

In this plant the blossoms are three *Gathered Picot Rings* that were worked closely in sequence.

Stem leaves are small *Picot Rings* and the ground leaves are *Catwalk Picots*. The grass is made with two very large *Reverse Picots* that are cut open after gluing and their tips then frayed with a needle.

The bud is a *Gathered Picot Ring*. Flower petals and ground leaves are *Over-Crocheted Picot Rings*.

93

These flowers each have seven petals of *Gathered Picot Rings After Closing the Ring*. They were worked with two different picot gauges. The ground leaves are two *Catwalk Picot Chains* that were twisted in different directions before gluing.

INSTRUCTIONS:

3-shuttle work, variegated pink, light and dark green .

Top Blossom: Three *Completely Gathered Picot Rings*

Center Blossom: Three *Partially Gathered Picot Rings*, 6 of 7 gathered.

Bottom Blossom: Three *Partially Gathered Picot Rings*, 4 of 7 gathered.

All flower petals were gathered *Before Closing the Ring* and the two green stem leaves *After Closing the Ring.*

VARIATIONS

1. Work five, six or seven petals and a pistil from reverse picots.
2. Add small leaves of *Josephine-* or *Picot Rings* between blossoms.
3. Make the leaves on the stem smaller and farther apart.
4. Use this stem as an element in a larger plant

MAGNOLIAS
3-shuttle work

The blossom petals were knotted in a circle as usual and tied together with a *Thread Scissors.* Part of the petals were flipped upwards and held in place by gluing.

The calyx and the branches were made with brown over pink and green threads.

WATER LILIES *(on painted silk)*

Some of the green leaves are *Over Crocheted* and others are *Gathered Picot Rings After Closing the Ring.*

New Ideas in Tatting
Part V
Mixed Tatting
Ideas to Further Spur Your Own Imagination

Pieces knotted bit by bit and laid onto foam-padded silk. Everything is held in place by glass and frame. All flowers and leaves, except the spikes, are explained in the previous chapters.

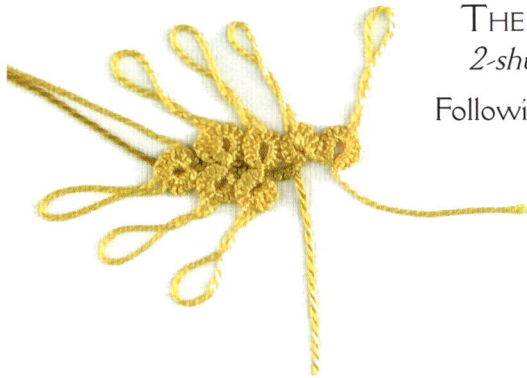

THE SPIKES
2-shuttle work

Following the first *Josephine Ring,* with a very large picot, two more were tatted right after each other and placed to the right and left of the second thread.

The long picots were cut open and their tips frayed with a needle prior to application on the silk background.

The background
is formed by two
colors of art board, all
elements secured with
a glue stick.

Both the yellow and pink flowers are made from two
blossoms placed on top of each other. The red one is a long
Catwalk Picot Chain that was coiled into shape.

A bouquet of an abundance of fantasy flowers,
using lace thread, glued onto art board.

This bouquet was tatted in lace thread and glued onto art board.

FLOWER BOUQUET

The blossoms are composed of small *Picot Rings* that are connected to each other and arranged in circles or half circles.

To form connections, pull thread through a picot of the previous ring, put shuttle through the loop and tighten loop, then secure with a half knot.

There are three types of flowers:

The yellow is worked like a doily in three rounds,

the purple flower uses two color changes in two half rounds and a final round in one color circles the previous two.

The red flower is worked in variegated thread.

99

These two flowers were worked in lace thread with *Picot Rings* that are connected to each other, similar to those on previous page.

For this "CLEMATIS" each petal starts in the center with a darker *Chain of Josephine Rings,* followed by continuously adding one *Picot Ring* after another in variegated pink thread while going around the center.

For the two lower petals, a *Chain of Picot Rings* was worked in muted lilac thread instead of a *Chain of Josephine Rings* to depict the start of wilting. Blossom is worked with one shuttle; leaves with two shuttles.

CLEMATIS

LILY

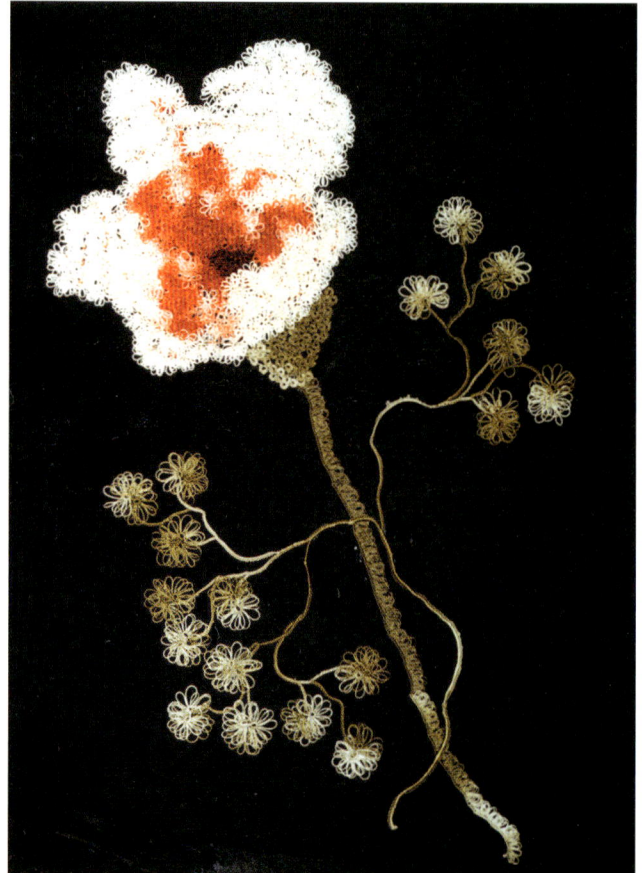

This lily is worked with 2 shuttles, white and orange, in order to design the calyx in a life-like fashion. One or two *Reverse Knots* had to be inserted between all *Picot Rings.*

A *Chain of Josephine Rings* forms the calyx.

Leaves consist of triple *Picot Rings,* their thread over tatted with another green thread to form the stem.

All threads of the stem were tied together, piece by piece with *Reverse Knots,* forming the long stem.

Tatting on Eggs
All tatting was attached with a glue stick.

To work with wire, combine the wire with a thread. This can be any type of thread or yarn, such as silk ribbon, fancy novelty yarn, mohair, or bouclé wool, etc. Overtat these two "threads" with *Reverse Knots* or *Picots*. It is best to use very thin wire doubled over in order to clamp the working thread into the wire loop.

Picots can be densely pushed together on the wire and the wire itself can be arranged in a three dimensional manner.

For this spike the upper large picots were cut open.

Question: Is the *Creative Knot* an important knot?

Answer: Yes. Each 2- or 3-shuttle work begins with it and each work is finished with it. Furthermore, one can add a new thread with the *Creative Knot* at any time.

Question: What is the difference between a *Creative Knot* and a *Split Creative Knot*?

Answer: To finish a 3-shuttle work, the first half of the *Creative Knot* can be worked over just one thread. This way the knot will not be so thick.

Question: When are *Reverse Knots* used?

Answer: For stems, stalks and small branches and for small flower pistils.

Question: Where do I use the *Double Knot*?

Answer: In creative tatting, the *Double Knot* is only used to form the *Picot Ring*.

Question: When do you use the *Thread Scissors*?

Answer: This enables you to clamp something between the left and right thread. For instance the first petal for closing a round of petals to form a blossom or a previously worked chain of tatted elements.

Question: What is a chain?

Answer: Working one element after the other with only one shuttle.

Question: How do I add a new thread?

Answer: Usually with a *Creative Knot* with the old and the new thread. In a row of *Reverse Knots*, as in a stem of a flower, one can just continue knotting with the new thread because these knots hold each other.

Question: What am I supposed to do with the starting and ending threads?

Answer: Before and after a *Creative Knot* threads can be cut off very short.

Question: When do I crochet over the *Picot Rings* for a flower from *Over Crocheted Picot Rings*?

Answer: Each *Picot Ring* will be *Over Crocheted* before the next ring is begun.

Question: When does one use 3 shuttles?

Answer: For all blossom and plant work.

Question: How many petals should a blossom have?

Answer: At least 5. If it has more, the pistil uses *Reverse Picots* instead of *Reverse Knots*.

Question: What can I work using just one shuttle?

Answer: All types of chains

Question: And what do I use those chains for?

Answer: For instance to design trees, or for bushes, clamp the chains with the *Thread Scissors* to add branches with foliage.

106

Index of the Knots and Elements

The Author

Helma Siepmann, residing in Germany was born in 1936. She learned classical tatting at the age of 14 and developed in 1987, after long years of practice, the novel free, creative tatting technique, as explored in this book. A technique which lends itself, in imaginative ways, to represent the freedoms of nature, requiring no strict, specific instructions.

Revolutionary, not only in the world of tatting, but in the overall world of freeform thread techniques, it enables each and everyone who dares to play with shuttle and thread to be an artist.

1980 - 1983	Instructor at adult education centers
1987	Development of creative tatting
1983 - 2001	38 national and international community exhibitions
1983 - 2001	26 publications national and international magazines
1985 - 2001	Active involvement in press, radio and TV programs
1987 - 2000	11 solo exhibitions
1987 - 2002	National and international training courses
1989	Book publication with Rosenheimer Verlagshaus, title "Kreatives Occhi"
1991	First place at the competition TEXTILKUNST INTERNATIONAL, Krefeld
1995	Workbook with OZ-Verlag, title "Creative Freizeit - Creatives Occhi"
1996	Co-founder of the DEUTSCHER OCCHI RING
1997 - 2002	Self publication (9 spiral bound books in German, 5 in English)
1998	Founder of the INTERNATIONALER OCCHI RING
1998 - 2000	Organizer of 3 international tatting meetings
1998 - 2001	National and international mail order distribution of work leaflets (bimonthly)
2001 - today	Editorial assistance for the craft magazine LENA
2001 - today	Work with groups on the internet
2002	Courses in Tokyo and Kyoto (Japan)
2002	"Innovative Tatting" book with Lacis, USA, English translation of "Kreatives Occhi"
2004	"Tatting, Artistry in Thread" book with Lacis, USA